S. Proctor.

CW01597493

Photocopiable Activity Book

Year 6 Non-Fiction Writing

by Sue Garnett

Introduction

Photocopiable Non-Fiction Writing for Year 6 is designed as an aid to the busy classroom teacher planning non-fiction writing activities for the Literacy Strategy.

The author has written a selection of non-fiction example texts covering the different genres required by the Literacy Strategy. These are accompanied by Writing Frames to help children to carefully plan and carry out their own piece of writing after study of each example.

For those children who struggle to think up ideas, or who have special needs, there are writing support sheets for each activity.

The main points to remember about each different type of non-fiction writing are summerised at the beginning of each section of the book. These may be enlarged and turned into wall posters to use as a constant reminder of the points made.

Topical Resources, P.O. Box 329,
Broughton,
Preston,
Lancashire.
PR3 5LT

Topical Resources publishes a range of Educational Materials
for use in Primary Schools and Pre-School Nurseries and Playgroups.

For the latest catalogue
Tel 01772 863158
Fax 01772 866153
e.mail:sales@topical-resources.co.uk
Visit our Website at:
www.topical-resources.co.uk

Illustrated by John Hutchinson & Paul Sealey

Typeset by Paul Sealey Illustration & Design,
3 Wentworth Drive, Thornton, Lancashire.

Printed in Great Britain for 'Topical Resources', Publishers of Educational Materials, P.O. Box 329, Broughton, Preston, Lancashire PR3 5LT by T.Snape & Company Limited, Boltons Court, Preston Lancashire.

First Published January 2002

ISBN 1 872977 64 2

Contents

Non-Fiction Year 6

Non-Fiction for Year 6 is designed to develop children's writing skills in non-fiction. This photocopiable book contains different types of non-fiction writing models and worksheets.

Aims

The book aims to improve children's writing skills by providing them with a model followed by a similar idea for them to write about using the framework provided, following the features of that writing.

How Does it Work?

The book is divided into different types of non-fiction writing. Within each type of writing there are several models each consisting of the example and two writing frames. Each group of three pages is laid out in a similar way.

First Page

- This is a model of the type of writing.
- The teacher reads the model with the children.
- The teacher discusses the model looking closely at the features of it, the grammar and vocabulary used and the layout.

Second Page

- This is a work page for children who need more support, ideas and guidance. The teacher will discuss the work sheet with the children in detail and help them complete it.
- The work sheet has information about the features of that type of writing. The teacher should read it through with the children.
- The worksheet has information about how to plan the ideas and set out the piece of writing. The teacher should explain how to use it.
- This worksheet has a word bank. It gives the children ideas and correct spellings to help them with their work.
- After the children have filled in the framework, they will use it to help them write their final piece of work which may be in an exercise book or on paper.

Third Page

- This is a work page which most of the children in the class will use to jot down their ideas before writing a final piece of work on separate paper. The teacher will discuss the work sheet before the children use it.
- The work sheet has information about the features of that type of writing. The teacher should read it through with the children.
- The work sheet has information about how to plan the ideas and set out the piece of writing. The teacher should explain how to use it.
- After the children have filled in the framework, they will use it to help them write their final piece of work which may be in an exercise book or on paper.

• POINTS TO REMEMBER •

Non-Chronological Reports

- Have a title.
- Have an introduction.
- Are factual e.g. "Claude Monet lived 1840-1926."
- Are written in paragraphs.
- May have headings and sub headings e.g. Monet, Renoir, Degas, Seurat.
- After the introduction, the paragraphs could appear in any order.

Impressionist Painters

The Impressionist painters were a group of artists who joined together for the purpose of mounting exhibitions in Paris during the eighteen hundreds because they did not like the work done by artists of their day. They had a very special style of their own and tended to paint in the open air and not the studio. They painted seascapes, summer in Paris and Parisian nightlife. They used the primary colours and introduced colour reflections into shadows.

Monet

Claude Monet lived 1840-1926. Monet was born to a wealthy family and he was brought up by the seaside in Normandy. The beautiful seaside inspired him to paint landscapes. He painted outside in all kinds of weather. When he was older he moved to Paris. His family brushed him aside and so he was very poor until his paintings began to sell when he was in his forties. One of his most famous paintings is called 'Waterlilies'.

Renoir

Pierre Auguste Renoir lived 1841-1919. He moved to Paris when he was three years old. Until the age of nineteen he painted porcelain pots. His paintings were joyful. They showed people having a fun time. He made his name when he was nearly forty. One of his most famous paintings is, 'The Luncheon of the Boating Party'.

Degas

Edgar Degas lived 1834-1917. He was a quiet, shy man who lived privately. He became an artist at the age of 18 and devoted his whole life to art. He liked to go to the opera and paint the young ballet dancers both on the stage and in the rehearsal rooms. One of his most famous paintings is, 'The Dancing Class'.

Seurat

Georges Seurat lived 1859-1891. He was born in Paris and became well known for his technique of painting in dots. He liked to paint on large canvases some of which were two and a half metres long. He spent most of his time on his own and he was so secretive that even his close friends did not know he had a wife or son. He died at the age of 39 from meningitis. One of his most famous paintings is, 'La Grande Jatte'.

How to Write a Non-Chronological Report

Writing Support Sheet

Name: ______________________ **Date:** ______________

Write your own non-chronological report about famous footballers or pop stars.

Features of a Non-Chronological Report

- Has an introduction
- Each paragraph may have a heading
- Each paragraph tells us something different
- You can swap the paragraphs around except for the introduction.

Planning Your Report

Title could be: – Famous Footballers
Introduction – what they do, teams, countries, competitions, goals scored etc.
Famous footballers ideas - e.g.
Heading 1 - Beckham,
Heading 2 - Owen
Heading 3 - Best

Title:

Introduction:

Heading:

Ideas:

Heading:

Ideas:

Heading:

Ideas:

Useful Ideas / Word Bank

football
team
scored
league
England
goal
competition

---

pop star
sang
school concert
gold disk
television
tour
music award

How to Write a Non-Chronological Report

Writing Frame

Name: ________________________________ **Date:** ________________

Write your own non-chronological report about a group of famous people e.g. writers, athletes, explorers.

Features of a Non-Chronological Report

- It has an introduction
- Each paragraph may have a heading
- Each paragraph tells us something different
- You can swap the paragraphs around except for the introduction.

Planning Your Report

Title – appropriate to your report

Introduction – generally, what they do

Headings – different person in each heading with information about them.

Title:

Introduction:

Heading:

Ideas:

Heading:

Ideas:

Heading:

Ideas:

Non-Chronological Report

Example 2

Cities in the USA

The United States of America is the fourth largest country in the world (nearly 40 times bigger than the UK). It is made up of 52 states and has many interesting cities to visit.

San Francisco

San Francisco is in western USA. It is in the state of California. It nestles in hills around the bay. It is famous for the Golden Gate Bridge which is a beautiful suspension bridge. The roads are so steep people use the cable cars to get from one place to another. At Fisherman's Wharf down by the marina you can buy fresh seafood. You can go by ferry to the abandoned island prison of Alcatraz from which no one ever escaped.

New York

New York is one of the largest cities in the USA. It has a population of seven million. Manhattan is an island. It is 13 miles long and there are many sky scrapers. This is where you will find the Empire State Building and the Statue of Liberty which you can get to on a short ferry ride. There are lots of shops here, theatres, galleries and museums. They have their own China town, Little Italy and Jewish quarter where people of these nationalities live.

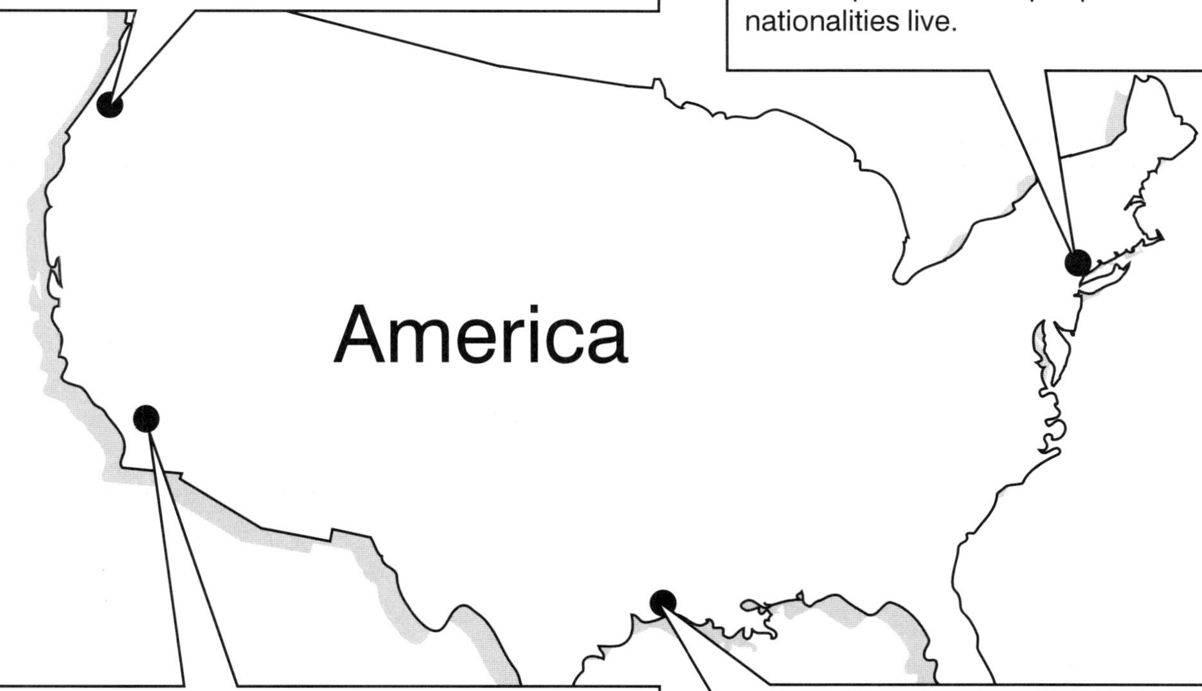

Los Angeles

Los Angeles is in California. It is famous for its movie industry and lots of famous movie stars live here. You can go to Mann's Chinese Theatre where famous people have left prints of their hands and feet in the pavement. You can take a tour around Beverly Hills where the rich and famous live. Los Angeles has hot sunny weather most of the year. Malibu and Santa Monica are sea side resorts where people work out, skate and surf. It is famous for the theme park Disneyland.

New Orleans

New Orleans is in Mississippi and at the mouth of the enormous Mississippi River. The French and the Spanish settled here. A lot of people visit the French quarter where jazz music plays all day and night. There are lots of beautiful old buildings here where the rich people used to live with their slaves. Each year there is a 'Mardi Gras' here when they have a parade. People dress up and you can see decorated floats. You can take a ride on a paddle steamer up the Mississippi River.

How to Write a Non-Chronological Report

Writing Support Sheet

Name: ________________________________ **Date:** ______________

Write your own non-chronological report about some of the towns and cities in the UK.

Features of a Non-Chronological Report

- It has an introduction
- Each paragraph may have a heading
- Each paragraph tells us something different
- You can swap the paragraphs around except for the introduction.

Planning Your Report

Title - Towns and Cities in the UK

Introduction – UK made up of countries, counties, cities, towns

Headings - where the town is, size, rivers, famous buildings, football grounds, museums, parks etc.

Title:

Introduction:

Heading:

Ideas:

Heading:

Ideas:

Heading:

Ideas:

Useful Ideas / Word Bank

London
Edinburgh
Cardiff
Manchester
Liverpool
Birmingham
Newcastle
Exeter

buildings
cathedral
castle
church
museum
zoo
park
river
theatre
shopping

entertainment
sport
shopping
culture

How to Write a Non-Chronological Report

Writing Frame

Name: ________________________________ **Date:** ________________

Write your own non-chronological report about some of the towns and cities in the UK.

Features of a Non-Chronological Report
- It has an introduction
- Each paragraph may have a heading
- Each paragraph tells us something different
- You can swap the paragraphs around except for the introduction.

Planning Your Report

Title - as appropriate

Introduction - general information about the UK

Headings - different town / city in each paragraph with information.

Title:

Introduction:

Heading:

Ideas:

Heading:

Ideas:

Heading:

Ideas:

The Vikings

The Vikings lived in Britain about 1000 years ago. They were from Norway, a land of mountains and fjords, where the winters were long and cold and it was difficult to grow crops. They were tall and fair haired and very fierce in battle.

Home Life

The men built boats and went hunting. They grew flax to make clothes. They grew wheat, rye and barley. They kept cows, sheep and horses. They also practised sword fighting and spear throwing. The women were always busy spinning and weaving. The women cooked and brewed strong beer. The children did not go to school. They played and learnt skills they would need when they were older.

Viking Long Boats

The Vikings built long boats. They were narrow with one sail. The front part curved up high into the shape of a bird's beak or an animal's head.
The men on board called their ships 'Dragons'.

Viking Raiders

The Vikings were raiders and every summer would set off across the seas in their long boats. They would steal anything of value and also take prisoners who would become their slaves. Before they left the villages, they would set them alight.

Life After Death

The Vikings believed in many gods. When they died they were buried with their belongings because they believed in the after life. When wealthy Vikings died they were buried in their warship with all their belongings, for example food and drink, weapons and their animals. Poor people were buried in a big hole in the ground with only a few things to take with them to the after life, for example spindles for weaving and a barrel of milk. If they were honourable and brave they would go to Valhalla, Viking heaven.

How to Write a Non-Chronological Report

Writing Support Sheet

Name: ______________________________ **Date:** ____________________

Write your own non-chronological report about a period in history.

Features of a Non-Chronological Report

- It has an introduction
- Each paragraph may have a heading
- Each paragraph tells us something different
- You can swap the paragraphs around except for the introduction.

Planning Your Report

Title – What period in history is it?

Introduction – Who is it about? When did they live? What was life like then?

Headings – choose three ideas from:
Home Life, Jobs, School, Entertainment, Fighting/Wars.

Title:

Introduction:

Heading:

Ideas:

Heading:

Ideas:

Heading:

Ideas:

Useful Ideas / Word Bank

Victorians
Tudors
Romans
Egyptians

century

home life
cooking
food
farming
animals
tools
grow

jobs
making
school
books
pens
chalk

How to Write a Non-Chronological Report

Writing Frame

Name: ______________________________ **Date:** ______________

Write your own non-chronological report about a period in history.

Features of a Non-Chronological Report
- It has an introduction
- Each paragraph may have a heading
- Each paragraph tells us something different
- You can swap the paragraphs around except for the introduction.

Planning Your Report
Title - appropriate to your report.

Introduction – generally about the people and life in your chosen period on history.

Headings - different aspects of their lives.

Title:

Introduction:

Heading:

Ideas:

Heading:

Ideas:

Heading:

Ideas:

• POINTS TO REMEMBER •

Explanations

- Are written in the present tense
  e.g. Heat some water in a pan.

- Use technical words
  e.g. molecules, magnify, microscope

- Are impersonal
  e.g. It cannot ..., Some people ...

- Use hypothetical language, which often includes observed facts
  e.g. If they ..., When they ...

- Use diagrams.

What makes things *hot* or COLD?

To find out what makes things hot or cold it is important to understand what things are made of.

Take a cracker and crumble it into pieces. Each piece still looks like a cracker. If a person looked at one little crumb under a microscope it would still look like a cracker. If however, they could magnify it millions of times, they would see that it is not just one crumb. Instead they would find out that it is a crowd of tiny specks darting around without stopping.

Each one of these tiny specks is a molecule. Molecules are always moving. Sometimes they speed up and sometimes they go slowly but they never stop. Every material in the world is made up of molecules.

When something is heated, the molecules move faster. When something is cooled, the molecules slow down.

Ask an adult to heat some water in a pan. Wait one minute, then ask them to test the temperature and then touch the water yourself. The heat has made the molecules move faster.

If the adult takes the water away from the heat, the molecules will slow down and the water will get cooler. If water is put in a freezer it will get cold and turn to ice. This is because the molecules are moving so slowly that they bump into each other and stick together in a hard lump.

Heat can even melt a piece of steel. If steel is heated up sufficiently the molecules speed up until they break away from each other and slide around. The steel is then soft enough to be made into other shapes. When the steel cools down it becomes hard again and holds its new shape.

How to Write an Explanation

Writing Support Sheet

Name: ________________________________ **Date:** ________________

Write your own explanation telling how you can change something from solid to liquid and from liquid to gas?

Features of Explanations
- Present tense
- Technical words e.g. molecules
- Uses words like - it, they
- Uses words like - if, when
- Uses diagrams (simple drawings).

Planning Your Explanation
Introduction – a simple sentence telling what you are about to write about.
Paragraph 1 – solid to liquid
Paragraph 2 – liquid to gas
Diagram - a simple drawing

Title:

Introduction:

Changes from solid to liquid Ideas:	Simple drawing:

Changes from liquid to gas Ideas:	Simple drawing:

Useful Ideas / Word Bank

solid to liquid

jelly (solid)

water

dissolves

becomes liquid

cool

solid again

liquid to gas

heat water

gas (steam)

cool

becomes liquid

evaporate

sets

freezes

How to Write an Explanation

Writing Support Sheet

Name: ______________________________ **Date:** ______________

Write your own explanation telling how you can change something from solid to liquid and from liquid to gas?

Features of Explanations
- Present tense
- Technical words
- Impersonal e.g. it, they
- Hypothetical language e.g. if, when
- Uses diagrams (simple drawings).

Planning Your Explanation

Introduction - tell what you are about to explain.

The two processes – what happened?
Why did it happen?

Conclusion

Title:

Introduction:

Process 1 Ideas:	Suggested diagram:

Process 2 Ideas:	Suggested diagram:

Conclusion

Why do leaves change colour in Autumn?

For most of the year leaves on plants or trees are green. Leaves contain a green colouring called chlorophyll. With sunlight, chlorophyll helps change water into food. The chlorophyll acts as a green pigment or colouring. Leaves also have a yellow pigment, which cannot be seen because it is hidden by the stronger green colour.

In Autumn the leaves stop making the green pigment, allowing the yellow colour to show through. Autumn leaves can also have red, orange or purple pigments that hide all or part of the yellow. However, these colours only appear if the days are bright and sunny and the nights are cool. That is why in some years, the leaves are brighter than in others.

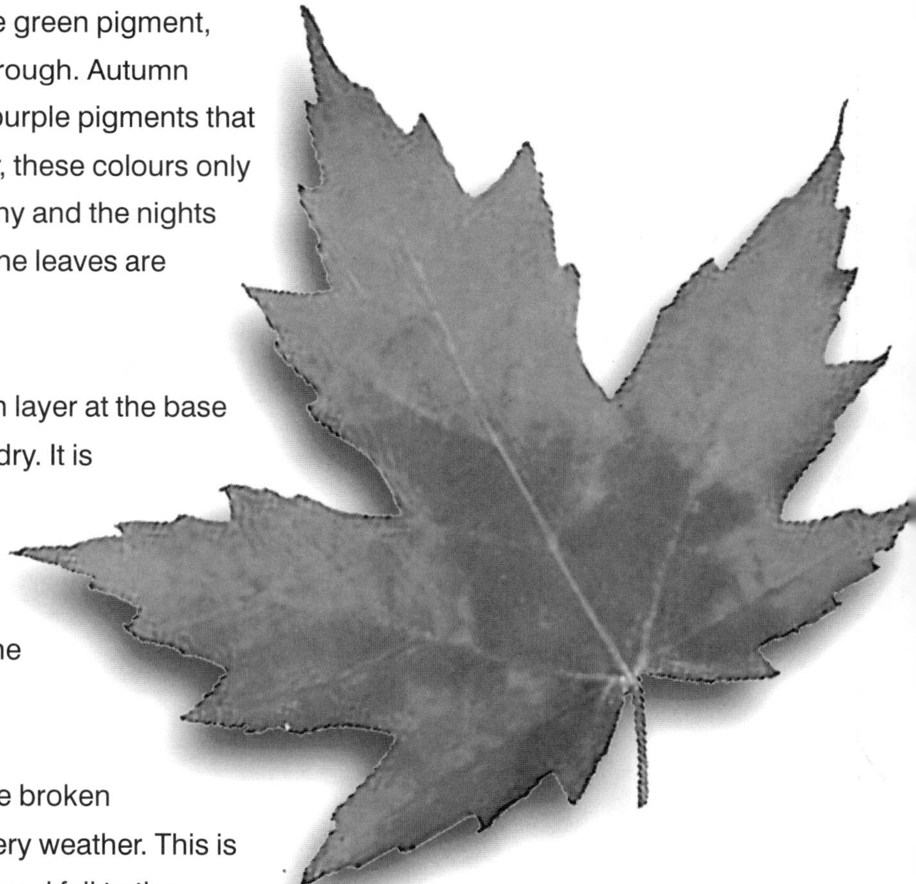

While the colours are changing, a thin layer at the base of each leaf stalk becomes hard and dry. It is like a dam that keeps food and water from flowing back and forth between the leaf and the tree. The leaf is now no longer a living part of the tree and eventually dies.

As the leaf is no longer living, it can be broken away from the tree by windy or showery weather. This is why leaves change colour in Autumn and fall to the ground.

How to Write an Explanation

Writing Support Sheet

Name: ______________________________ **Date:** ______________

Write your own explanation telling why plants need water and light.

Features of Explanations

- Present tense
- Technical words e.g. pigment
- Uses words like - it, they
- Uses words like - if, when
- Uses diagrams.

Word Bank

Why plants need water:
Plants take water from soil, travels up the stem, – without water it will die.

Why plants need sunlight:
Leaves contain colouring called chlorophyll. Chlorophyll changes water into food, without it plants will die.

Why do plants need water and light?

Diagram:

How to Write an Explanation

Writing Frame

Name: ______________________ **Date:** ____________

Write your own explanation telling why plants need water and light.

Features of Explanations
- Present tense
- Technical words
- Impersonal e.g. it, this
- Hypothetical language e.g. if, when
- Uses diagrams.

Title: ______________________

Why do plants need water?	Diagram:

What happens if there's no water?	Diagram:

Why plants need sunlight?	Diagram:

What happens if there's no sunlight?	Diagram:

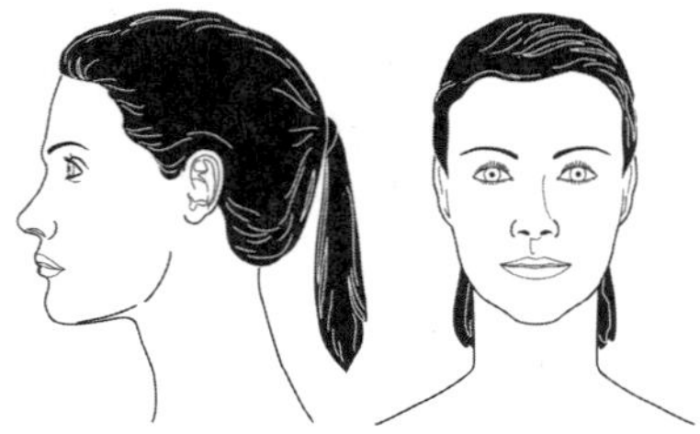

How do people taste things?

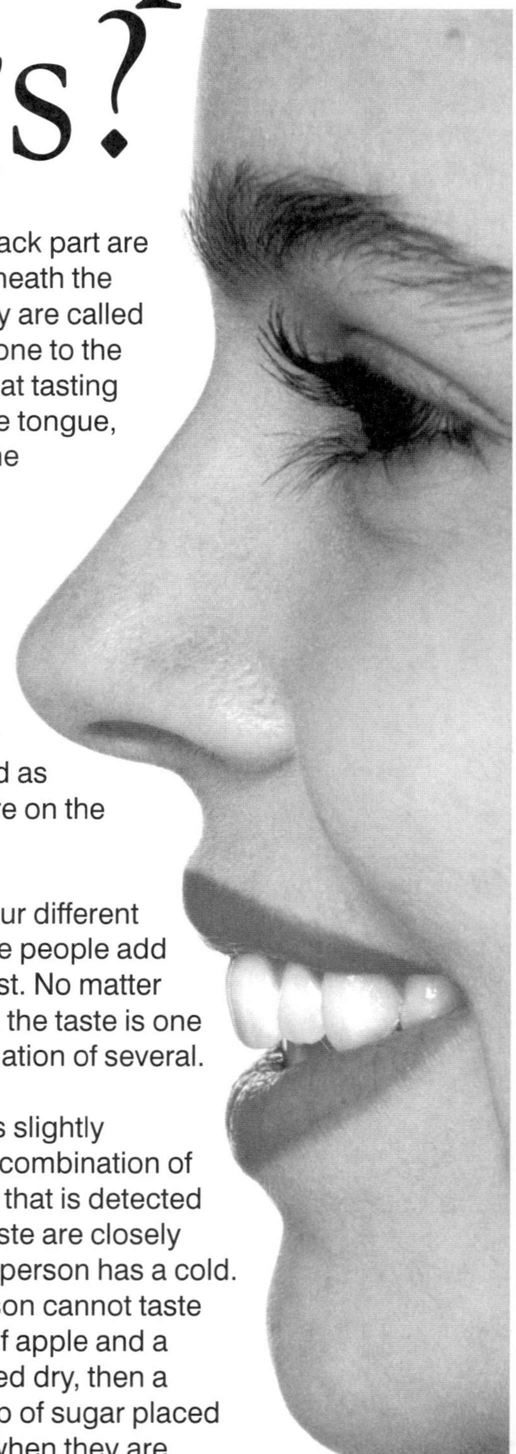

Tasting begins in the tongue. Its tip and edges and back part are dotted with little bumps that have holes in them. Beneath the holes lie small knobs that look like flower buds. They are called taste buds and long threads called nerves connect each one to the brain. The buds on different parts of the tongue are good at tasting different things. Salty and sour are tasted at the side of the tongue, sweet at the front of the tongue and bitter at the back of the tongue.

If a person puts a drop of syrup on the tip of their tongue, the syrup drips through the holes onto the buds. Signals go quickly along the threads to the brain and identify 'sweet'. If a person puts a drop of syrup on the back of the tongue, they won't taste this, because the buds at the very back detect only bitter things. If a drop of vinegar is put on either side of the tongue it will be identified as 'sour'. The buds that detect salty things are on the front and the sides.

Sweet, bitter, salt and sour are the four different tastes that everyone agrees on. Some people add soapy and metallic tastes to the list. No matter what is put in the mouth, the taste is one of these or a combination of several.

The flavour of food is slightly different. It can be a combination of tastes plus an odour (smell) that is detected by the nose. The smell and taste are closely linked. This is evident when a person has a cold. If the nose is very stuffy, a person cannot taste the difference between a piece of apple and a piece of onion. If the tongue is wiped dry, then a person will not be able to taste a lump of sugar placed in the mouth. Things can be tasted only when they are dissolved in a liquid, such as saliva.

How to Write an Explanation

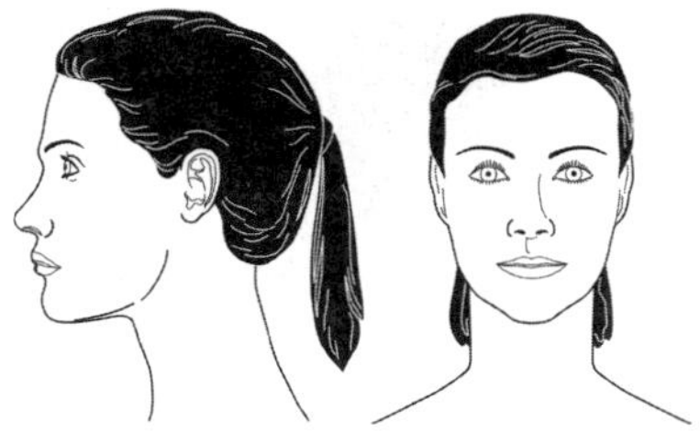

Writing Support Sheet

Name: ______________________ **Date:** ______________

Write an explanation about how the ear enables a person to hear.

Features of Explanations
- Present tense
- Technical words e.g. nerves
- Uses words like - it, they
- Uses words like – if, when
- Uses diagrams.

Planning Your Explanation

Introduction – simple sentence telling what you are writing about.

Explanation – important words telling exactly what happens.

Title:

Introduction:

Explanation:

Diagram:

Useful Ideas / Word Bank

How we hear:
- Sound waves (vibrations) fill the ear
- Outside of ear acts like a funnel
- Stretched across the funnel is a skin like that on a drum. Sound waves make it vibrate.
- Vibrating ear drum moves a bone that is touching it. The bone moves another bone and then another. Last bone sets up waves in a liquid.
- Waves make thousands of tiny hairs move back and forth. The hairs are connected to the brain. The brain identifies the sound.

How to Write an Explanation

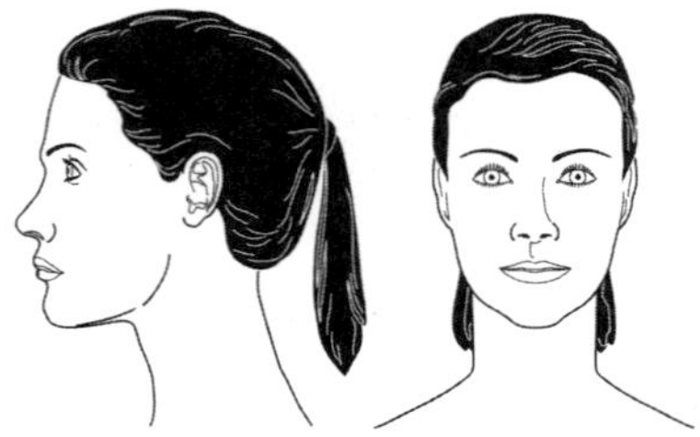

Writing Frame

Name: ______________________________ **Date:** ______________

Write your own explanation about how one of your senses work.

Features of Explanations
- Present tense
- Technical words
- Impersonal e.g. it, they
- Hypothetical language e.g. if, when
- Uses diagrams.

Planning your Explanation

Introduction – opening sentence

Process – explain using technical words, and impersonal language

Title:

Introduction:

Explanation: Ideas:	Diagram:

• POINTS TO REMEMBER •

Autobiographies

- Are written in the first person
  e.g. I always enjoyed...

- May consist of facts and opinions
  e.g. 'I won my first ever prize.' (fact)
  'They weren't impressed.' (opinion)

- Are written in the past tense
  e.g. When I was eleven...

- Include the most important and interesting events.

Biographies

- Are written in the 3rd person
  e.g. He spent... When Robbie was six...

- May consist of facts and opinions
  e.g. 'He started to walk.' (fact)
  'He was bright.' (opinion)

- Are written in the past tense
  e.g. He shouted... They flew...

- Include the most important and interesting events.

Autobiography
(Diary Writing)

Example 1

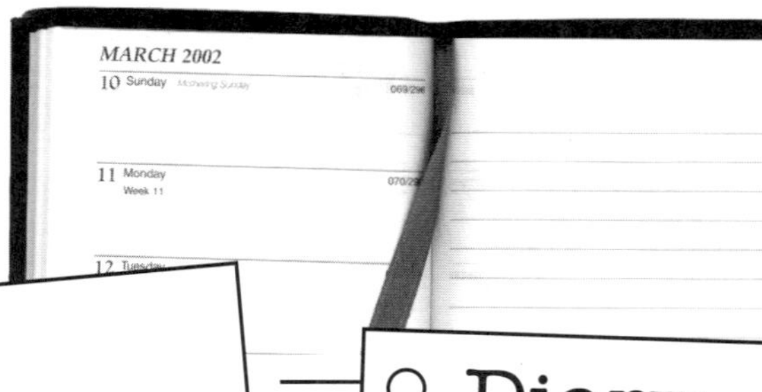

Diary

Kelly's diary – Residential
Holiday to Abbotsmere

Monday 7th June
Today our class went on a residential holiday to Abbotsmere. Thirty children and three teachers set off on the bus with parents lining the road. We're staying in a hostel by the lake. All the children are in dormitories and I'm with Becky and Jane. I chose the top bunk.
After our evening meal we played rounders on the field. Then we had a midnight feast!

Diary

Tuesday 8th June
Didn't get much sleep last night. Jane snored all night!
In the morning we went mountain biking.
It was great fun going up the winding tracks into the mountains. Sarah fell off her bike but she was okay. We saw loads of rabbits and a deer.
In the afternoon we went canoeing.
It was brilliant.
We had to put the canoes together and walk over them.
Nearly everyone fell in!
After tea we had a treasure hunt.

Diary

Wednesday 9th June
Today we all went orienteering. John our instructor showed us how to use a compass. Our group lost ours and had to be given another. It took us ages to find all the points and we were the last group back. It's not surprising though because we went paddling in the lake!

We had a barbecue for tea. I had four hot dogs!

Diary

Thursday 10th June
In the morning we went grass sledging. It's even better than on snow and you don't get wet. Mrs Jones went head first into some nettles. She was covered in stings. Ryan hit a tree and ended up with a lump the size of a golf ball on his head. We had a picnic by the lake at lunch time.

After lunch we packed our things and set off home. It was the best holiday I've ever had.

Autobiography How to Write a Diary

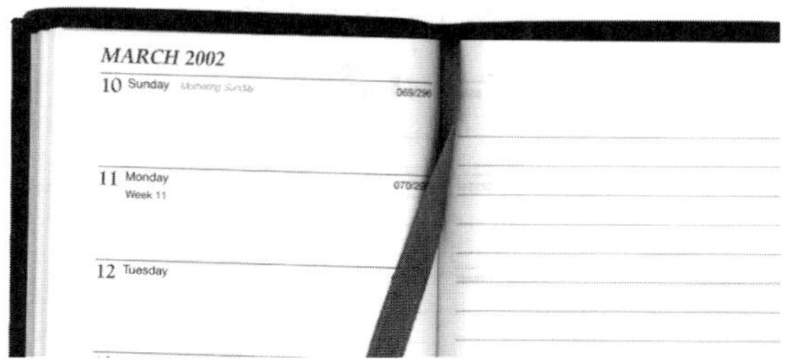

Writing Support Sheet

Name: ______________________________ **Date:** ________________

Write your own diary. It could be true, or you could make it up.

How to Write a Diary

Write the title

Write the dates for each page

Remember the audience is the writer i.e. YOU!

Day 1 date:

Ideas:

Useful Ideas / Word Bank

Holiday

Who went - family, class, cubs, guides?

How did you get there - car, bus, train?

What was the place like - busy, quiet?

What was the weather like - sunny, hot, cloudy?

What did you do - swim, fun fair, visit restaurants, beach, castle?

OR

Christmas

OR

Going into hospital

OR

When someone special died/pet died

Who is the diary about?

What did you do?

Where? home, hospital, garden, street?

How did it make you feel? sad, happy?

Day 2 date:

Ideas:

Day 3 date:

Ideas:

Autobiography How to Write a Diary

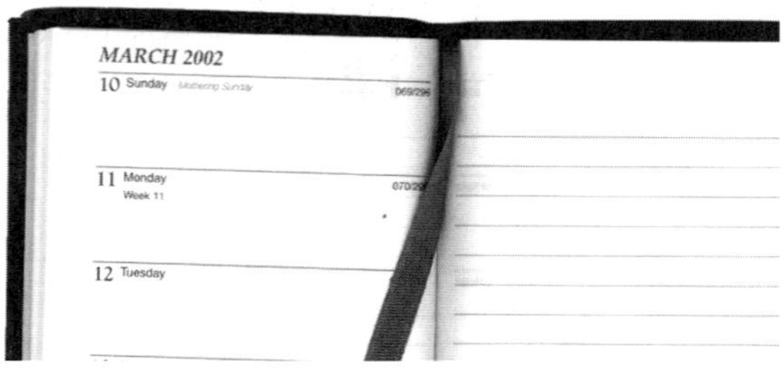

Writing Frame

Name: ______________________________ **Date:** ____________________

Write your own diary. It could be real or you could make it up.

How to Write a Diary
Write the title
Write the dates for each page
Remember the audience is the writer i.e. YOU!

What could you write a diary about?
A holiday, or a special event (happy or sad).

Think about – who? when? where? what?

Day 1 date:

Ideas:

Day 2 date:

Ideas:

Day 3 date:

Ideas:

Day 4 date:

Ideas:

Slaving Over a Hot Stove

Excerpts from Oliver James' Autobiography - Celebrity Cook

Chapter 1

I always enjoyed cooking, even as a toddler. I'd stand on a stool by my mum's side and watch her for hours. She was a brilliant cook and she always let me stir the mixtures and try it out too! I especially enjoyed eating cake mixture and one day while she was answering the phone I ate all the cake mixture and licked the bowl clean. We didn't have cakes that day!

When I was three years old I made breakfast for everyone in the house, mum, dad, Greg my older brother, Timmy the baby and Jack my pet dog. I gave them all the same – orange juice, cereal, milk and fresh raspberries in ONE bowl! They weren't impressed. The only one to eat it all was Jack (he was sick for three days afterwards and died shortly after that! Although I'm sure that was of old age.)

Chapter 2

When I was eleven we had a cake competition at school. None of the boys entered except for me (it wasn't cool.) My entry looked like a castle and it was made of lots of sponge cakes of different sizes. It was decorated with coloured icing and it had a moat around it. I won my first ever prize that day. The Headmaster said it was the best cake he'd ever seen. I had to stand at the front during the presentation while the Headmaster gave me a massive cookery book. From that day on I vowed to become a chef when I was older and work in a London hotel.

Chapter 3

When I was eighteen I left home and went to London. I lived with my auntie and uncle near Battersea power station. I didn't like London at first, it was nothing like my home town; it was noisy and the pace of life was fast. I got a job in a hotel kitchen. I worked hard and soon I was in charge making my own recipes. People came from all over the country to try them. My finest moment was winning chef of the year and being presented with the award on television in front of my family. They were really proud of me. I was lucky, I got to do what I enjoyed most and earn lots of money too. Even now that I'm retired you'll still find me slaving over a hot stove and still enjoying it!

How to Write an Autobiography

Writing Support Sheet

Name: ______________________ **Date:** ______________

Write your own life story (autobiography). Imagine you became famous.

Features of an Autobiography

- Use the word 'I'
- Write facts and opinions
- Write it in the past e.g. played
- Write about when you were a - baby / child / adult
- Write about the most exciting events.

Planning Your Autobiography

Chapter 1 –some things you did when you were a baby / toddler

Chapter 2 - what you did when you were a child

Chapter 3 - what you did when you were an adult.

Title:

Chapter 1

Chapter 2

Chapter 3

Useful Ideas / Word Bank

baby

toddler

child

teenager

adult

afterwards

although

achieved

became

famous

proud

How to Write an Autobiography

Writing Frame

Name: ______________________________ **Date:** ____________________

Write your own autobiography. Imagine that you are a famous celebrity.

Features of an Autobiography
- Write it in the 1st person – I
- Write facts and opinions
- Write it in the past tense e.g. walked
- Write about different stages in your life
- Write about important moments.

Planning Your Autobiography

Chapter 1 – as a baby/toddler

Chapter 2 - child

Chapter 3 - adult

Chapter 1

Chapter 2

Chapter 3

Water Baby

A biography of Robbie Goldsmith By Laura Unsworth

Robbie was a special boy born to be a swimmer. He was bright, lively and a born optimist. When it was his fourth birthday he had a party in his back garden. Everyone had to bring their swimming things. He spent the whole time in the paddling pool and even ate his birthday cake in there. 'Look I can swim!' he shouted to everyone, splashing about. Robbie had never been to the swimming baths. His parents were older, his father was in a wheelchair and his mother suffered badly from asthma so they had difficulty taking Robbie places. However, when he started swimming lessons, Robbie was a natural; he loved the water. He wasn't afraid of anything and was always prepared to have a go. By the time he started school he could swim 25m.

When Robbie was six he joined the local swimming club. It was called The Otters. He was very competitive. In his first competitive race he came second. "Don't worry Laura, I'll win next time," he said determinedly. He did win the next race; in fact he never lost a race after that. Every morning Robbie went to the pool before breakfast. He swam until his arms and legs ached and only stopped when it was time for school. Soon Robbie was swimming for his county and winning all the competitions.

When Robbie was twenty he was selected to swim for his country in the Olympic Games. Although his parents were ill, they flew out to Australia to see him win the final. His proudest moment was receiving the gold medal in front of them. "Like I said Laura, I told you I'd win," he said, with a cheeky grin on his face.

How to Write a Biography

Writing Support Sheet

Name: ______________________________ **Date:** ______________

Write a biography about a child in your class who has become famous for playing sport.

Features of a Biography

- You should use he or she, not I
- Write about when they were a baby, child and then adult
- Write what the person said and use speech marks.

Planning Your Biography

Introduction – what they became famous for

Paragraph 2 – as a baby/toddler

Paragraph 3 – child

Paragraph 4 – adult and achievements

Title:

Introductory Paragraph:

Paragraph 2 - Baby / Toddler

Paragraph 3 – Child

Paragraph 4 – Adult/ Achievements

Useful Ideas / Word Bank

football
athletics
swimming
tennis
running

competitive
keen

practised
competitions

medals
first

succeeded

champion
represented
country
famous

How to Write a Biography

Writing Frame

Name: ________________________________ **Date:** ________________

Write a biography about a child in your class who has become a famous sporting celebrity.

Features of a Biography

- Write it in the 3rd person i.e. he or she
- Write about the different stages in the person's life
- Include quotations
- Include facts and opinions.

Planning Your Biography

Introduction – what they became famous for

Paragraph 2 - Baby / Toddler

Paragraph 3 - Child

Paragraph 4 – Adult/Achievements

Title:

Introductory Paragraph:

Paragraph 2:

Paragraph 3:

Paragraph 4:

• POINTS TO REMEMBER •

Journalistic Reports

- Are about events which interest the public.
- Select and present the information carefully.
- Explain points clearly.
- Give lots of information.
- Are written in a balanced and ethical way.

Journalistic Report

Example 1

Frayshire Evening Post

Tuesday 4th August **1st Edition**

Nuisance Dogs on Rampage

Report by A. Barker

The townsfolk of Harchester were afraid to come out of their houses because of a pack of rampaging dogs in the town.

Parents were keeping children indoors after several frightening incidents in Avenham Park.

Alex Redhead and Ben Garnett were playing football in Avenham Park when they heard the dogs barking. The dogs chased the boys across the park. The boys managed to climb a nearby tree but had to wait an hour before the park keeper arrived. He chased the dogs away with a water gun. Although the boys were unhurt they were very shocked by the incident.

Just a day later a father and son flying their kite were attacked by the same dogs. The kite was ripped to pieces and the father had his trousers torn quite badly.

"Something has got to be done about those dogs," said the park keeper. "People should be able to feel safe in the park, and that's not the case any more."

The dog warden has since rounded up the dogs, all of which were strays. They have been taken to the RSPCA until homes are found for them.

How to Write a Journalistic Report

Writing Support Sheet

Name: ______________________________ **Date:** ______________

Write your own newspaper report about something happening in your town.

A Good Journalist
- Writes about what the public is interested in
- Thinks about both sides of a story and what is right
- Writes information carefully.

Planning Your Report
- Write a headline
- Use the 4 Ws – when? where? who? what?
- Use a quotation (what someone said)
- Include a picture if you have room.

Idea for a headline -

When?

Who?

Where?

What?

Useful Ideas / Word Bank

The local park
- no equipment
- rubbish
- broken
- teenage gangs
- muggings
- fights

Vandalism
- teenagers
- children
- broken windows
- glass
- rubbish
- car thefts
- car radios / CD players
- joy riding

Thieving
- shops
- cars
- bikes

How to Write a Journalistic Report

Writing Frame

Name: ______________________ **Date:** ______________

Write your own newspaper report about something happening in your town.

A Good Journalist

- Writes about events which interest the public
- Selects and presents information carefully.
- Writes in a balanced and ethical way.

Planning Your Report

- Write a headline
- Write a brief introduction
- Use the 4 Ws - Who? What? Where? When?
- Include a quotation.

Ideas for a headline –

When?

Who?

Where?

What?

Don't forget the quotation!

Childhood Stress!

Report to the Government

by Jan Redmond, retired School Inspector, Hopbourne

Childhood stress is on the increase. Questionnaires, filled in by seven to eleven year olds have shown conclusively that the children of our generation show significant signs of stress.

From the age of four, as soon as children enter school they develop tell tale signs of stress. The teachers, pressured by Government intervention, test children as soon as they walk through the door. Although the curriculum focuses on learning through play, the teacher knows that by the age of seven children will have to take tests set by the Government. Children become increasingly aware of the urgency to get through the curriculum and practise in the style of the tests. They become stressed by parents who are encouraged to hear them read every night, practise their times tables and spellings and complete practice papers.

By the time children are eleven years old, they have been used to taking annual tests, in exam conditions. They are warned about the tests months before by their teachers. They are given practice tests to do at home. They even practise the tests at school in exam conditions just to give them a flavour of what it is really like. By the time the tests come children are extremely stressed.

The children show their stress in different ways. At school if they are struggling with the work they can become introverted, sometimes afraid to speak in case they get the answer wrong. At playtime they keep themselves to themselves feeling a failure. Bright children can feel pressured to do well. If they are really stressed they can switch off and go into a world of their own. At home, they can become awkward, arguing with parents about homework, stamping feet and slamming doors. They can withdraw into their bedrooms only coming out when it is time for school. They can develop sleeping problems, even wetting the bed. They can sometimes develop eating problems because of worry. Occasionally they can get into trouble outside the home, stealing, breaking windows etc. due to anger and frustration.

The survey showed that children have little time to play with friends, chat together, ride bikes or play on their computers. Their lives revolve around tests. When questioned in the survey about how they would like to bring up their own children, the view was conclusive. Children should have more time to relax, watch TV and play.

How to Write a Journalistic Report

Writing Support Sheet

Name: ______________________________ **Date:**________________

Write your own journalistic report to the Government about childhood stress caused by other children.

A Good Journalist
- Writes about what the public is interested in
- Thinks about both sides of the story and what is right
- Writes their information carefully.

Planning Your Report
- Write a clear headline
- Write a simple introduction
- Think of 3 important points
- Write a conclusion summing up your report.

Title:

Name of reporter:

Introduction:

Point 1:

Point 2:

Point 3:

Conclusion:

Useful Ideas / Word Bank

stress caused by children -
- smoking
- behaving badly in school
- truanting
- stealing
- vandalism
- designer clothes

what happens if a child doesn't fit in -
- called names
- battered
- no friends
- clothes ripped
- poisonous phone calls or letters

how it affects the child -
- don't go out
- truant
- fail exams
- eating problems
- sleeping problems

How to Write a Journalistic Report

Writing Frame

Name: ______________________ **Date:** ______________

Write your own journalistic report to the Government about childhood stress caused by peer pressure.

A Good Journalist

- Writes about events which interest the public
- Selects and presents information carefully
- Writes in a balanced and ethical way.

Planning Your Report

- Write a simple introduction
- Write 3 main points
- Think about:
  - the cause of stress
  - what happens if a child doesn't fit in
  - how it affects the child.

Title:

Reporter:

Introduction:

1st point

cause

what happens

how it affects the child

2nd point

cause

what happens

how it affects the child

3rd point

cause

what happens

how it affects the child

Conclusion

Kid'sTime Television *Film Censorship*

"Hi! This is Tim Henderson reporting for Kid's Time Weekly News.

Well, it's holiday time again and I've been out on the streets of Lipingham all day trying to find out just what children do during the holidays. However, what I've found out is a real problem affecting the children of today. Of course they do the usual things like swimming, ice skating, football in the park and going to the cinema. However, this is where the problem begins. I was outside the Roxy and spoke to several unhappy members of the public. Apparently, they're unhappy with the film censorship as it stands. One family who were hoping to see 'Space 11', were turned away because their youngest son Adam is only eleven and the rating is a twelve. Dad and older brother Jamie went in without him leaving a very unhappy mother and son outside. Some teenagers who were hoping to see 'Teen Tear Away' were turned away because they weren't eighteen and yet the film is aimed at teenagers. What the people cannot understand is why there is this censorship when children can watch any film they like at home.

We spoke to the Film Censorship Board and they were adamant that censorship was necessary. They told us that the children of today need to be protected from films unsuitable for their age. When we questioned them about the fact that children can and do watch whatever they like at home on television or on video they declined to comment. So children, unless you're the age you need to be to watch a film at the cinema then don't try to get in or you'll be very disappointed.

This is Tim Henderson reporting for Kid's Time Television Weekly News. Next week we'll be reporting on kids and computers. Until then, that's all from me. Goodnight."

How to Write a Journalistic Report

Writing Support Sheet

Name: ______________________________ **Date:** ________________

Write a report to be read out on TV about children and computers.

Good Journalists
- Write about what people are interested in
- Give lots of information.

Planning Your Report
- Think of a title
- Write a clear introduction
- Give lots of facts and information.

Title:

Who are you?

Who are you reporting for?

What are you going to talk about?

Problems- affects on children's lives:

Names of people you spoke to :

Conclusion:

Useful Ideas / Word Bank

Types
- PC's
- game boys,
- play stations

Cost
- from less than £100 to over a thousand
- games from £5 upwards

Time spent
- most nights
- weekends,
- at school

How it affects lives
- don't have any other hobbies
- don't talk to others
- don't talk to families
- hurts their eyes
- don't get fresh air
- get unfit
- nothing else to talk about.

How to Write a Journalistic Report

Writing Frame

Name: ____________________ **Date:** ____________

Write a commentary for TV on children and computers.

Good Journalists

- Talk about what interests the audience.
- Give lots of information
- Explain their points clearly.

Planning Your Report

- Title - as appropriate
- Clear introduction
- Include lots of facts and information
- Names of people interviewed
- Conclusion – sum up points.

Title:

Who are you?

(Introduction) What are you going to talk about?

Information/facts:
(types of computers, cost, time spent on them)

Problems/How it affects lives:
(no hobbies, don't communicates, unfit etc)

Conclusion / Summary:

• POINTS TO REMEMBER •

Points of View

- Have an introduction
- Are logical, and have an easy to follow plan
- Use words that move the argument on
  e.g. Firstly... Finally...
- Reach a conclusion
  e.g. To conclude...
- Use examples to prove a point
  e.g. ...health risks that include cancer.

Balanced Reports

- Consider both sides of the argument
- Summarise competing views
  e.g. Is it better? Is it worse?
- Analyse strengths and weaknesses
  of different positions
- Use examples to prove a point.

Pimlingham School
Duchess Lane
Tetherington
Henshire
10th January 2002

Mobile Phones!

Dear Parents

A very serious problem has arisen at school during the past few months. More and more children are bringing mobile phones to school. The Governors and I have considered the problem and have decided that as from Monday of next week, mobiles phones will be banned. If any are found on a child's person or on the premises, then they will be confiscated.

Firstly we are banning mobile phones because of the disturbance they cause during lessons. It is very difficult for the teacher to talk over the sound of a mobile phone ringing and furthermore the sound also disturbs children while they are working.

Secondly we are banning mobile phones because they can be easily lost or stolen. Mobile phones are appealing to all children and if seen lying around will, no doubt, be picked up by others. Furthermore, they are easily lost due to the fact that they are so small.

Finally, we are banning mobile phones because of the health risks associated with them. You will have no doubt read articles in newspapers about the health risks that include cancer and tumours especially to children whose brains are not fully developed.

To conclude, we think that this is the appropriate measure to take. We will of course always allow children to make phone calls from the office when necessary and continue to pass messages onto your children when you telephone us.

Yours sincerely

K Evans

K Evans
Headteacher

How to Write a Letter Giving Your Point of View

Writing Support Sheet

Name: ________________________________ **Date:** ________________

Write a letter to the Headteacher disagreeing with the decision to ban mobile phones.

Writing a Letter

- Address on the right hand side followed by the date
- Dear Sir or Madam
- Paragraphs
- Write Yours faithfully at the end
- Write your full name.

Planning Your Letter / Point of View

- Write an introduction
- Write one point per paragraph
- Use words like – firstly, secondly, finally, therefore, however
- Sum up at the end.

Opening paragraph:

2nd paragraph:

3rd paragraph:

4th paragraph:

5th paragraph (conclusion):

Useful Ideas / Word Bank

Points which would be useful if you were arguing for mobile phones

- can use right away
- small - keep in your pocket/bag
- stops parents worrying
- in case of emergency - 999, police,fire, - ambulance
- don't use school phone - less cost to school
- don't need coins

How to Write a Letter Giving Your Point of View

Writing Frame

Name: ______________________ **Date:** ______________

Write a letter to the Headteacher disagreeing with the decision to ban mobile phones.

Writing a Letter
- Address on the right hand side followed by the date
- Dear Sir or Madam
- Write in paragraphs
- Write Yours faithfully at the end
- Write your full name.

Planning Your Letter / Point of View
- Write an introduction with a brief explanation
- Write each point in detail backing up your comments with facts
- Use words like firstly, furthermore, however, although
- Summarise your views in the conclusion.

Ideas / Points for each paragraph e.g. convenience, size, no money needed, emergency, worry

1st paragraph (Introduction):

2nd paragraph:

3rd paragraph:

4th paragraph:

5th paragraph (Conclusion):

Letter to the Mayor - Conversion of Yew Tree Pond to a Supermarket

4 Rose Tree Gardens
Yewtown
Greenshire
15th May

Dear Sir,

I am writing to you about the possible conversion of Yew Tree Pond to a supermarket.

I have only recently moved into the area from London and I am definitely in favour of the conversion. Furthermore I am now on the committee of the Young Wives Club who are very keen to see the supermarket built.

Firstly, I am of the opinion that a supermarket would be a great asset to the town. At the moment there are no supermarkets in the town. Although there are many small shops the prices are extremely high, whereas a supermarket would bring the weekly shopping bill down by a substantial amount.

The second reason I am in favour of the supermarket is that it would save me time driving to 'Toptree' to get my shopping and I would save a lot of money in petrol.

My final reason for having the supermarket is that it would bring wealth to the town. A supermarket would not only bring new employment; moreover it would also mean that other people would come to the town and not only go to the supermarket, but visit the other shops and facilities as well.

Finally, I have enclosed a petition with fifty signatures from the Young Wives Club who are in favour of the supermarket. With so many people keen to see this happen it would be a great pity if it was turned down. I look forward to your reply.

Yours faithfullly
J Whitehead
Judith Whitehead (Mrs)

How to Write a Letter Giving Your Point of View

Writing Support Sheet

Name: ______________________ **Date:** ______________

Write a letter to the Mayor telling him why the pond should stay.

Writing a Formal Letter

- Address at the top right hand side and date
- Dear Sir or Madam
- Paragraphs
- Yours faithfully at the end.

Planning Your Letter/Point of View

- Write a short introduction
- Write 1 point per paragraph
- Use words to move the argument on e.g. firstly, secondly, finally
- Write a conclusion.

1st paragraph (Introduction):

2nd paragraph:

3rd paragraph:

4th paragraph:

5th paragraph (Conclusion):

Useful Ideas / Word Bank

Reasons for the pond to stay:

- **Environment**
  - kill all the wild life,
  - no beauty spot
- **Pollution**
  - cars
  - fumes
- **Traffic**
  - congestion
  - slow people's journeys
  - road rage
  - danger to children and old people
  - noise pollution

How to Write a Letter Giving Your Point of View

Writing Frame

Name: ____________________ **Date:** ____________

Write a letter to the town Mayor giving your reasons for not having a supermarket built on the site of Yew Tree Pond.

Writing a Formal Letter

- Address at the right hand side and date
- Dear Sir or Madam
- Write in paragraphs
- Yours faithfully at the end
- Write your full name.

Planning Your Letter/Point of View

- Write an introduction with a brief explanation
- Write each point (one per paragraph) in detail backing up your comments with facts
- Use words to move the argument on e.g. therefore, moreover, although
- Summarise at the end.

Ideas - e.g. environment, pollution, traffic etc.

1st paragraph (Introduction):

2nd paragraph:

3rd paragraph:

4th paragraph:

5th paragraph (conclusion):

Letters to the Editor
Umbria Evening Post

Family Life - Better or Worse?

Family life has changed since I was a boy. Is it better? Is it worse? In the fifties and sixties families sat at the dining table to have tea. Nowadays families sit in front of the television with a plate on their knees, or a take-away in a cardboard box or a plastic tray, not knowing how to use a knife or fork. However, they get to try food from around the world and they also learn how to use a remote control and set the video channel for their TV programmes.

In days gone by the family shared the household chores like washing up or hanging out the washing. Nowadays, dish washers, dryers and microwave ovens have changed life beyond recognition. In the sixties you'd have to wait a couple of hours for tea, nowadays you can have a casserole in ten minutes and throw away the carton afterwards without washing up which is great for the working mum with very little spare time.

In the evenings families played games together like cards or draughts, mums, dads, grandparents and children all joining in. Nowadays children don't know how to play games like Snakes and Ladders, Ludo or Tiddly Winks but their fine motor skills are evident when you see them use a computer or play station.

On Sundays the whole family dressed up in their best clothes and walked to church. The church was full and everyone knew the hymns. Nowadays, some people don't go to church for maybe a year or so, however they can join in a service in the comfort of their lounge. Sunday lunch was always enjoyed with a roast dinner and apple pie or steamed pudding. Nowadays, people don't even know how to bake a cake. However, they don't need to when supermarkets are open every day, sometimes twenty four hours a day and sell everything they need including tasty puddings at a reasonable price.

Times have changed, people have changed. Families enjoy life in different ways. Is it better? Is it worse? I don't know about that. Whatever happens, as long as families stick together and support one another it doesn't matter how they do it.

By Tom Watts, pensioner.

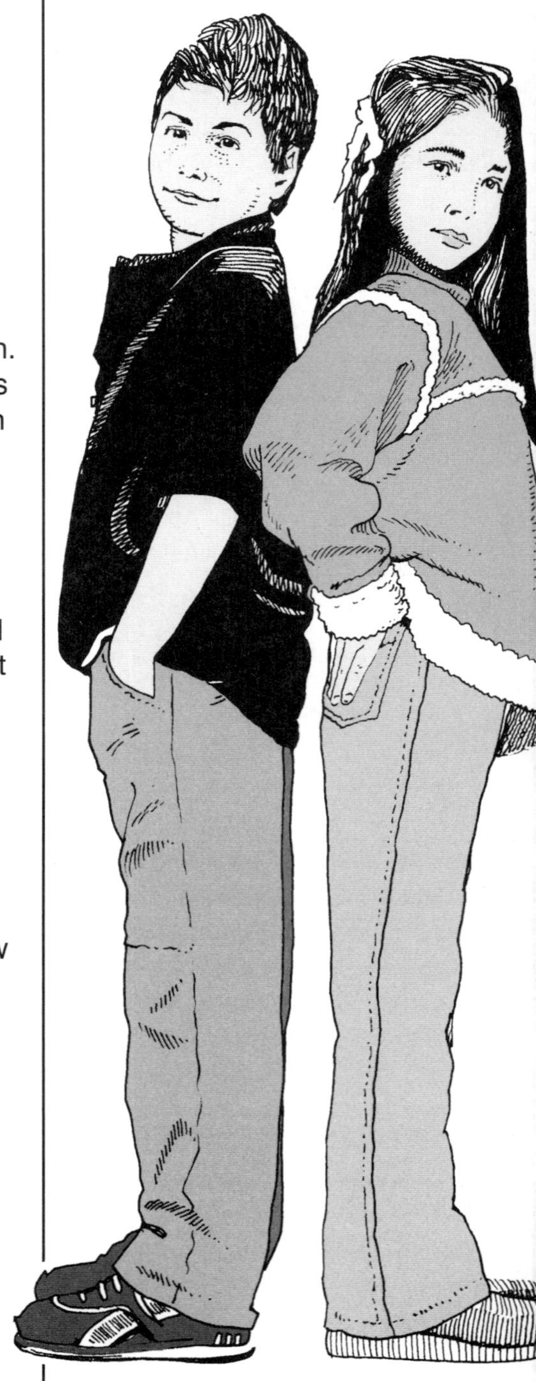

How to Write a Balanced Report Giving Different Points of View

Writing Support Sheet

Name: ______________________________ **Date:** ______________

Write a balanced report on the good and bad points of school now, and as it was many years ago.

A Balanced Report
- looks at both sides of the argument
- tries to be fair.

Planning Your Balanced Report
- Write an introduction
- Write each point looking at both sides of the argument
- Summarise at the end

Introductory paragraph:

2nd paragraph:

3rd paragraph:

4th paragraph:

5th paragraph (Conclusion):

Useful Ideas / Word Bank

School Now
uses ICT, equipment

school dinners

central heating

indoor toilets

use pen and paper

punishment by exclusion

School Then
no electrical equipment

went home for dinner

coal/wood fire

outdoor toilets

used chalk and boards

punishment by cane, slipper.

How to Write a Balanced Report Giving Different Points of View

Writing Frame

Name: ______________________________ **Date:** ____________________

Write a balanced report on how school has changed for better and worse.

A Balanced Report
- Considers both sides of the argument.
- Summarises competing views.
- Analyses strengths and weaknesses of different positions.

Planning Your Balanced Report
- Write an introduction
- Write each point considering both sides of the argument
- Summarise at the end in the last paragraph.

Ideas – comforts, equipment, punishments etc.

1st paragraph (Introduction):

2nd paragraph:

3rd paragraph:

4th paragraph:

5th paragraph (Conclusion):

• POINTS TO REMEMBER •

Legal Language

- Uses formal vocabulary
  e.g. forename, date appointed
- Uses headings and sub headings
  e.g. Date of Birth, Address, Progress Report
- Is usually written in the second person
  e.g. Does your child...?
- Provides spaces for answers or comments
- Has short sentences - clear and to the point
- Uses vocabulary appropriate to the audience who will be reading it
- May have open and closed questions
- May have bold type to make the important words stand out.

Education Department – Application for teaching post

At St James' CE Primary School, Wenlock

1. Personal

Surname: Daly

Forename(s): Angela

Date of birth: 19.11.70

Home address: 25 Sanderson Street
Wartington

Telephone no: 0164 386741

Post Code: WT5 4GR

2. Present Position

Present post: Teacher

Date appointed: 01.09.92

School: St Andrew's CE Primary, Brassington

Age range: 4-11

☐ Single sex ☑ Mixed

3. Education

St Winifred's CE Primary School, Wartington
Hancock High School, Wartington
Blacknook College, Blacknook

4. Qualifications

GCSE'S – English, Mathematics, French, History
Geography, Art, Science, ICT
A levels – English, Mathematics, French

Signature: A Daly

Date: 24.01.02

How to Write a Legal Language Form

Writing Support Sheet

Name: ______________________________ **Date:** ______________

Imagine you are an adult. Write your own form for a job at your school. Fill it in.

Features of a Form
- Be very precise
- Write headings
- Write sub headings
- Provide space for the answer to be written.

Planning Your Form
- What job is the form for?
- What information do you need to collect?
- Who will read this form?

Education Department

Application for:

1. Personal Information:

2. Present Position:

3. Education:

4. Qualifications:

Useful Ideas / Word Bank

What is the job for?
teacher
teaching assistant
secretary
welfare assistant
cleaner
caretaker

Personal
surname
date of birth
home address
post code
telephone number

Present position
present post
school
age range

Qualifications
GCSEs
A levels

How to Write a Legal Language Form

Writing Frame

Name: ______________________________ **Date:** ______________

Imagine you are an adult. Write a form for a position at your school. Fill it in with imaginary information.

Features of a Form
- Be precise
- Use formal language
- Use headings/sub headings
- Provide space for the answer to be written.

Planning Your Form
- Write all the subheadings underneath each other
- Fill in the answers
- Include lots of facts
- Imagine the audience is adults

Application for which job?

Name of school?

Personal information:

Present position:

Education:

Qualifications:

School Questionnaire for Parents

Confidential

Are you happy with the education your child is receiving? ☑ **Yes** ☐ **No**

Comment
I'm very happy with the education at school. All my children attended and they have done very well.

Is your child happy at school? ☑ **Yes** ☐ **No**

Comments *They like coming to school.*

Is the school well led and managed? ☑ **Yes** ☐ **No**

Comments *The school is very well organised.*

Is your child expected to work hard and do their best? ☑ **Yes** ☐ **No**

Comments –

Does the school cater for children with special needs? ☑ **Yes** ☐ **No**

Comments
My eldest child was helped with his reading.

Are the children well behaved at school? ☑ **Yes** ☐ **No**

Comments
The children seem to behave well in school but I have heard bad language and seen fighting outside.

Does your child get the right amount of work to do at home? ☑ **Yes** ☐ **No**

Comments
Sometimes my child gets too much homework especially at weekends. It would be better spaced out.

Do you feel happy to approach the school with problems? ☑ **Yes** ☐ **No**

Comments *The teachers are always pleasant and helpful.*

Does the school provide extra curricular activities? ☑ **Yes** ☐ **No**

Comments
There aren't many activities in winter.

Are there clubs for parents to attend? ☑ **Yes** ☐ **No**

Comments
I've attended the keep fit class and computer class. They're brilliant and I've made new friends too.

How to Write a Legal Language Questionnaire

Writing Support Sheet

Name: ______________________________ **Date:** ______________

Write a questionnaire for your friends to find out what they think about your school. Now fill it in.

Features of a Questionnaire

- They help people find out about something
- The questions are clear and to the point
- You may have to write yes or no
- You may have to write a comment.

Planning Your Questionnaire

- Write a list of questions the children would like to answer.
- Think of questions where the children would make a comment.
- Use as few words as possible for the questions.

Title:

Questions (think of comments)

1

2

3

4

5

6

Useful Ideas / Word Bank

happy

bullying

teacher

headteacher

interesting

lessons

clubs

activities

trophies/cups

equipment

test results

How to Write a Legal Language Questionnaire

Writing Frame

Name: ______________________________ **Date:** ________________

Imagine you are the Headteacher. Write a questionnaire to find out what children think about school and fill it in.

Features of a Questionnaire

- They provide people with information.
- They are clear and to the point
- They may have open and closed questions.

Planning Your Questionnaire

- Write a list of questions to interest children
- Think of questions which require a comment
- Use as few words as possible for the questions.

Title:

Questions (think of comments)

1

2

3

4

5

6

Wensley Vale Primary School

Report for School Doctor

Name of child Kevin Hargreaves

Date of birth 30.10.93

Address 5 Waterside Gardens
Witherington
Pentshire

Disability No use of legs (in a wheel chair)

Progress report

Kevin has been at our school since the age of four. At the age of seven he was involved in a car accident. He has lost use of both his legs.

Kevin is a bright boy and achieves well above the national average in test scores. He continues to make excellent progress with his work.

Kevin has adapted well to using his motor powered wheel chair and has access to all the classrooms in the junior department. He is able to access the playground using the new ramp that has been built. However, he has to be carried to the hall for assemblies as there are too many steps and he is unable to participate in PE and games at a class level. His parents are aware of the problems and are hoping that the school can consider building a ramp from the classroom to the hall.

T Harper

T Harper (Special Needs Co-ordinator)

How to Write a Legal Language Report

Writing Support Sheet

Name: ____________________ **Date:** ____________

Imagine you are a teacher. Write a report for a child who can not see very well.

Features of a Report
- Use formal language
- Uses headings and sub-headings
- Are clear and precise.

Planning Your Report
- Think about problems children may have.
- Use paragraphs to separate your ideas.
- Explain the support the child receives.

Name of school:

Who is the report for?

Name of child:

Date of birth:

Address:

Difficulty:

Progress report :

(positives/negatives)

(the support the child receives)

Name of person writing the report:

Useful Ideas / Word Bank

Problems -
lack of resources

needs one to one help getting about school

needs one to one support during play times.

cannot join in with reading activities

cannot join in with PE without support.

Help Given -
teaching assistant part time

support from outreach teacher for the blind

extra resources - braille books audio tapes.

How to Write a Legal Language Report

Writing Frame

Name: ______________________________ **Date:** ______________

Imagine you are a teacher. Write a report for a child who is partially sighted.

Reports
- Use formal language
- Uses headings and sub-headings
- Are clear and precise
- Use vocabulary appropriate for the audience who will be reading it.

Planning Your Report
- Think about some of the problems the child may have and jot them down
- Write each point in one paragraph
- Explain what support the child receives.

School?

Who is the report for?

Name:

Date of birth:

Address:

Difficulty:

Progress report :
(list the things the child does)

(list the support the child receives)